Kilmanns
Time-Gap
Survey

RALPH H. KILMANN
AND ASSOCIATES

Distributed by
KILMANN DIAGNOSTICS
1 Suprema Drive
Newport Coast, CA 92657
www.kilmanndiagnostics.com
info@kilmanndiagnostics.com
949.497.8766

TIME-GAP SURVEY

Introduction

This survey is designed to pinpoint the areas in your work life in which you might not be making the best use of your time. While there are many things (and people) that take your time, this instrument presents 35 key aspects of organizational life that have an impact on performance and morale. Once you have responded to the 35 items in this survey, you will be able to score and plot your time-gaps: those specific areas in which you should **change** the amount of time you spend on tasks and activities in order to increase your contribution to your organization's goals.

Response Scale

Carefully study the response scale below. You will be asked to use the three letters on this scale to record your responses to the 35 items in this survey. To ensure an accurate assessment, please keep these three letters clearly in mind while you respond to each item. You may refer back to this page at any time.

L   I should be spending **less time** on this task or activity than I am now in order to increase my contribution to my organization's goals.

R   Presently, I am spending the **right amount of time** on this task or activity. In fact, if I were to spend less or more time on it than I am now, my contribution to my organization's goals would decrease. *Note:* In some cases, the right time could be *no time*, especially if the task or activity hinders goal achievement.

M   I should be spending **more time** on this task or activity than I am now, so I can increase my contribution to my organization's goals.

TIME-GAP SURVEY

Instructions

For each item below, please circle the letter that indicates whether you should be spending *less time (L)* or *more time (M)* than you are now in order to increase your contribution to your organization's goals. If you are already spending the *right time* on the item in question (which could be no time), then circle the middle letter *(R)*.

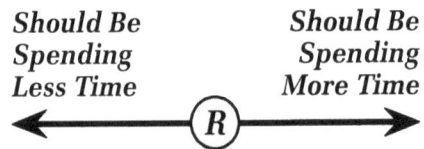

	Should Be Spending Less Time ←	*R*	*Should Be Spending More Time* →
1. I actively foster trust in my organization by speaking very positively and respectfully about other groups and departments.	L	R	M
2. I switch back and forth from task to task or project to project, which makes it difficult for me to bring the most important things to completion.	L	R	M
3. To resolve problems and improve teamwork, I actively encourage my fellow employees to have open and forthright group discussions.	L	R	M

TIME-GAP SURVEY

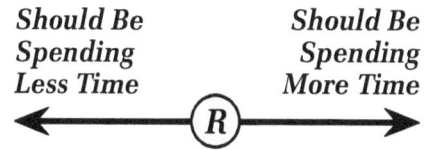

	Should Be Spending Less Time ←	(R)	Should Be Spending More Time →

4. I meet with my boss to clarify my objectives and priorities (especially after organizational goals or departmental responsibilities have been modified).

      L   *R*   *M*

5. I strive to improve my performance (*instead of* worrying about how I am viewed in my organization).

      L   *R*   *M*

6. I find myself duplicating the work of other groups and departments (because I don't fully trust them or the quality of their work).

      L   *R*   *M*

7. At the start of every day, I first plan and prioritize my activities and detail what I expect to accomplish by the end of the day.

      L   *R*   *M*

8. I find myself "reinventing the wheel" since I ignore how my team members solve similar work-related problems.

      L   *R*   *M*

TIME-GAP SURVEY

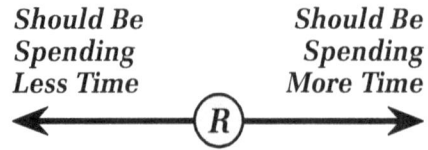

	Should Be Spending Less Time	← R →	Should Be Spending More Time

9. I directly contact and work with the departments that can provide the information or services that I need (*instead of* complaining or relying on the formal channels).

        L   R   M

10. I find myself worrying about what salary increase or bonus I will get this year or complaining about what I received last time.

        L   R   M

11. I actively encourage my coworkers to put aside past injustices and to focus on the future of the organization.

        L   R   M

12. I find myself having to restart my work because I allow phone calls, mail delivery, or unannounced visitors to break my concentration.

        L   R   M

13. I help my coworkers pinpoint the things that block our performance, so we can improve our teamwork.

        L   R   M

TIME-GAP SURVEY

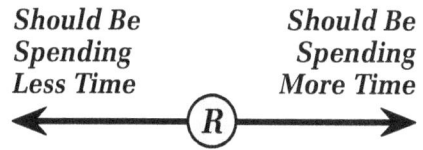

			Should Be Spending Less Time		Should Be Spending More Time
			←	Ⓡ	→
14.	I learn about the objectives and responsibilities of other groups and departments in the organization.		*L*	*R*	*M*
15.	I try to improve my chances for job transfer or promotion by doing my assigned job and learning new skills.		*L*	*R*	*M*
16.	When something goes wrong, I try to find out which person or group was at fault—so the finger won't be pointed at me.		*L*	*R*	*M*
17.	I reflect on my long-term value to the organization and try to crystallize my job priorities for the future.		*L*	*R*	*M*
18.	My team revisits and rehashes previous discussions and decisions because we keep our true opinions from one another.		*L*	*R*	*M*

	Should Be Spending Less Time	ⓇR→	Should Be Spending More Time

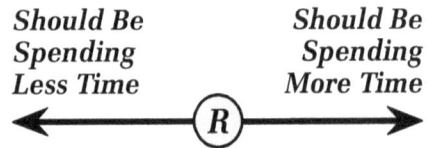

19. To make sure I am doing the right things, I periodically review the goals of my organization, department, and work group.

    L   *R*   *M*

20. I try to keep up to date on the stated criteria for performance reviews and how the review process works.

    L   *R*   *M*

21. I consistently focus my attention on working effectively with other groups (*in spite of* past misunderstandings, mishaps, or mistrust).

    L   *R*   *M*

22. I find myself procrastinating or day dreaming—and thereby ignoring the task directly in front of me and not getting it done.

    L   *R*   *M*

23. I draw the quieter members into our group discussions so that all possible views are examined and considered.

    L   *R*   *M*

TIME-GAP SURVEY

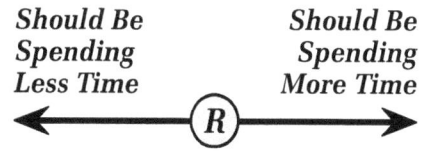

	Should Be Spending Less Time ←—(R)—→ Should Be Spending More Time		

24. I find myself complaining about all the unnecessary paperwork and procedures that are part of my job responsibilities.

       L   *R*   *M*

25. I regularly ask my boss for a review of how I am doing, so that I know what I should be doing differently in order to improve my performance.

       L   *R*   *M*

26. I diligently handle requests from other work groups and departments (because such attentive and timely responses promote trust and good will throughout the organization).

       L   *R*   *M*

27. By consistently asserting myself when my coworkers drop by for a friendly chat (by saying, for example, "not now, please"), I can complete my high-priority work on time.

       L   *R*   *M*

	Should Be Spending Less Time	←—(R)—→	Should Be Spending More Time

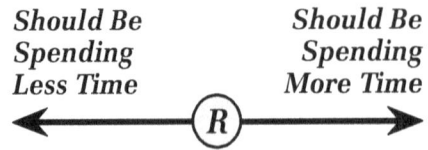

28. I regularly share my ideas with the members of my group in order to promote cooperation and teamwork.

    L   R   M

29. I periodically ask my boss to clarify company policies or procedures (*rather than* proceeding with my work only to discover that I didn't understand what was expected).

    L   R   M

30. I find myself worrying about the results of my performance review, which distracts me from getting my work done.

    L   R   M

31. I actively strive to build trust in my organization by quickly responding to requests for information and services that come from other departments.

    L   R   M

32. I work on the first task or problem that greets me—ignoring my job priorities for the day.

    L   R   M

TIME-GAP SURVEY

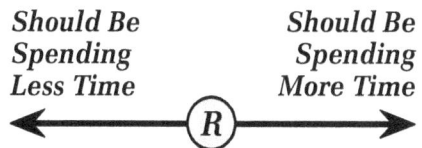

	Should Be Spending Less Time	(R)	Should Be Spending More Time

33. I actively encourage my coworkers to be team players in order to help one another get the whole job done.

    L   R   M

34. I keep up to date on strategic plans, long-term forecasts, and where my organization is headed, so that my work is on course with the future.

    L   R   M

35. I regularly talk with my boss and other key members of the organization in order to understand the criteria being used to assess my job performance.

    L   R   M

Scoring Your Responses

On the following page is your scoring sheet. Just circle the **L/M** in the appropriate column for every **L or M** that you circled on the survey. (Only L and M are scored, not R.) You will find it easiest to transfer your responses—in order—from 1 through 35.

For each column on the scoring sheet, sum the number of L/Ms that you circled. The resulting sums are your scores for five **time-gaps:** Cultures, Skills, Teams, Strategy-Structures, and Reward Systems. The meaning and implications of these time-gaps will be provided shortly.

TIME-GAP SURVEY

1. L/M	2. L/M	3. L/M
6. L/M	7. L/M	8. L/M
11. L/M	12. L/M	13. L/M
16. L/M	17. L/M	18. L/M
21. L/M	22. L/M	23. L/M
26. L/M	27. L/M	28. L/M
31. L/M	32. L/M	33. L/M

Sum: Cultures	Sum: Skills	Sum: Teams

4. L/M	5. L/M
9. L/M	10. L/M
14. L/M	15. L/M
19. L/M	20. L/M
24. L/M	25. L/M
29. L/M	30. L/M
34. L/M	35. L/M

Sum: Strategy-Structures	Sum: Reward Systems

Graphing Your Time-Gap Profile

The five scores that you just obtained can be summarized as a Time-Gap Profile. This profile shows your five scores plotted in bar-graph form for easy interpretation.

On the following page, please transfer each of your five scores (from the previous page) to the unshaded space provided on the right side of the graph—across from its associated time-gap on the left side of the graph. Naturally, it is essential that you accurately transfer your five scores.

On the top and bottom of the graph, you will see numbers ranging from 0 to 7. For each of your five time-gap scores (ignoring any 0 scores), fill in the bar graph from its corresponding hash marks to the 0 point on the far left—as illustrated below:

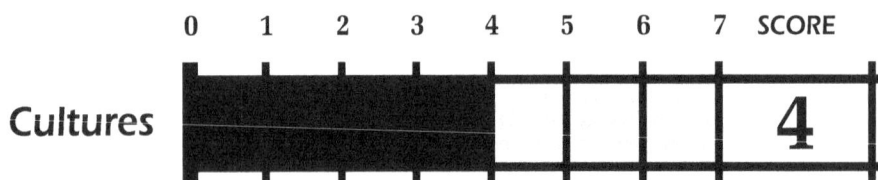

```
        0    1    2    3    4    5    6    7   SCORE

Cultures ████████████████████              4
```

My Time-Gap Profile

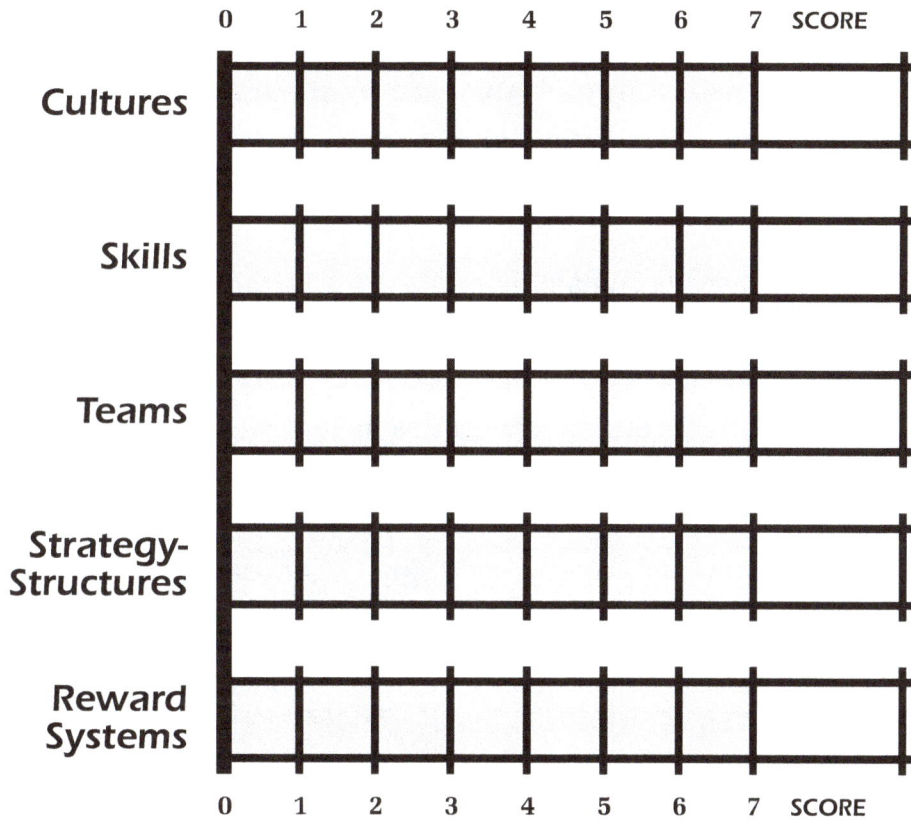

	0	1	2	3	4	5	6	7	SCORE
Cultures									
Skills									
Teams									
Strategy-Structures									
Reward Systems									
	0	1	2	3	4	5	6	7	SCORE

TIME-GAP PROFILE

Developing Organizational Profiles

Once all the individuals in your work group have obtained and graphed their scores on the five time-gaps, collect their numbers together on a separate sheet of paper so you can calculate five averages for Cultures, Skills, Teams, Strategy-Structures, and Reward Systems. Remember to divide the sum of the scores for each time-gap by the right number of individuals in your group: those who actually provided their scores for these calculations.

Once the five averages have been calculated for your work group, please enter the results in the appropriate spaces on the opposite page. Then, as you did for your individual scores, plot the averages for **1. My Work Group**. Next, if you have access to the other work groups in your department, you can calculate and plot the four averages for **2. My Department**. And if you have access to all the departments in your organization, you can also calculate and plot the four averages for **3. My Organization**. For your convenience, subsequent pages provide these graphs, including a space to enter the number of respondents (N) included in the analysis. *Note:* In calculating these various profiles, you might find it necessary to weight the averages of each group by the number of its members to adjust for different sizes of groups and departments in your organization.

1. My Work Group (N = _____)

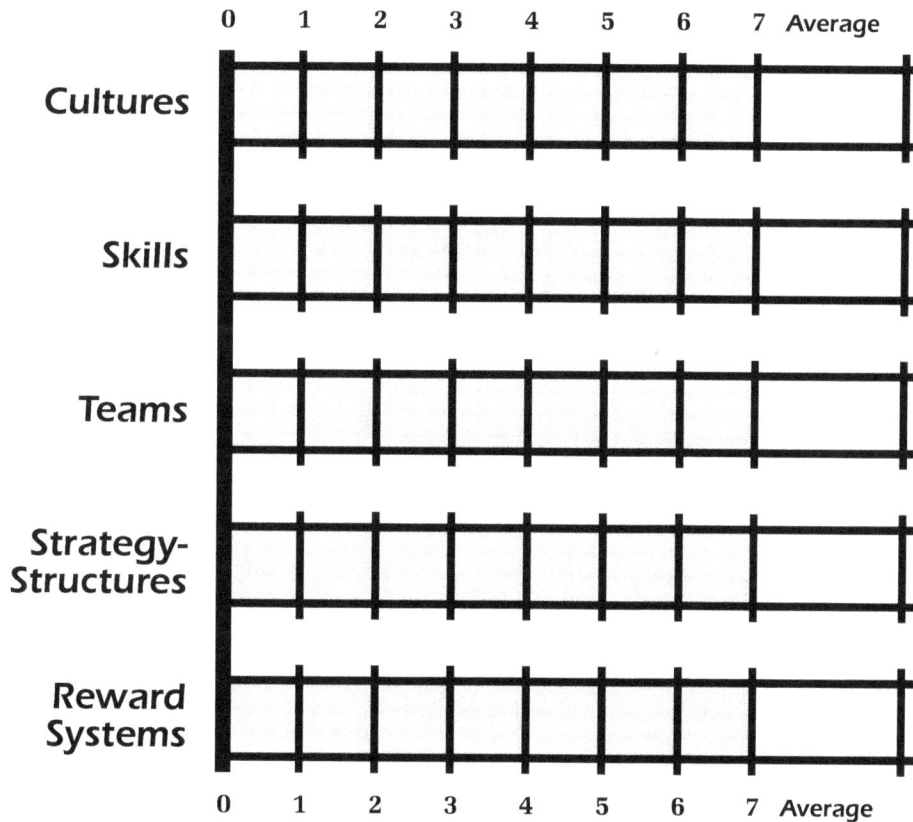

	0	1	2	3	4	5	6	7	Average
Cultures									
Skills									
Teams									
Strategy-Structures									
Reward Systems									
	0	1	2	3	4	5	6	7	Average

TIME-GAP PROFILE

2. My Department (N = _____)

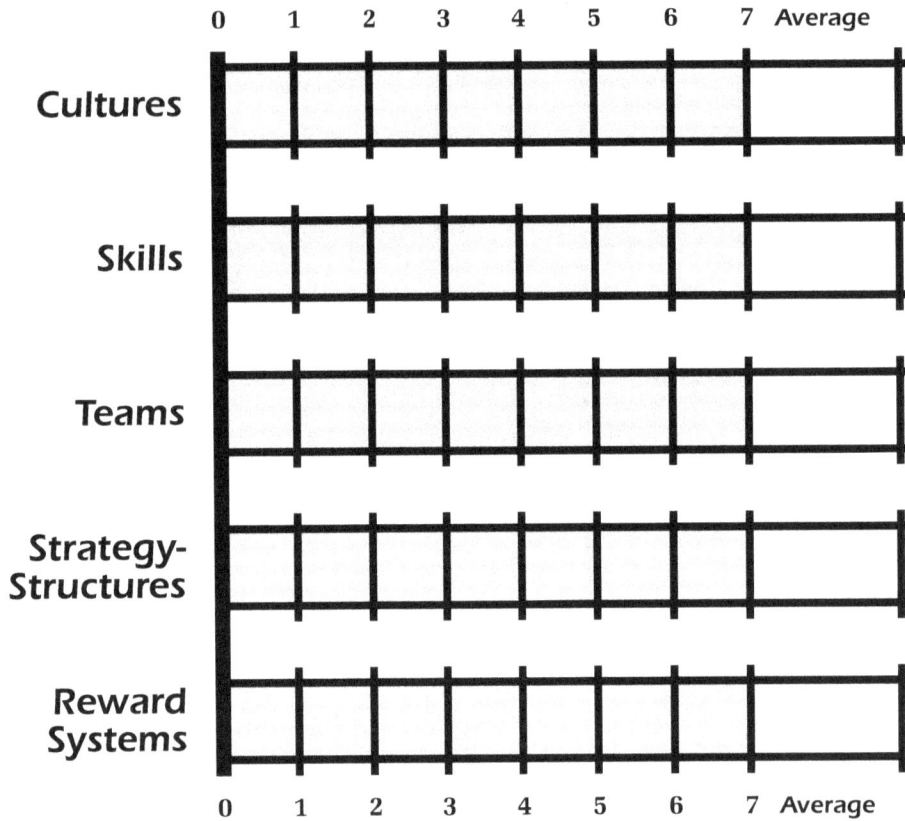

	0	1	2	3	4	5	6	7	Average
Cultures									
Skills									
Teams									
Strategy-Structures									
Reward Systems									
	0	1	2	3	4	5	6	7	Average

TIME-GAP PROFILE

3. My Organization (N = _____)

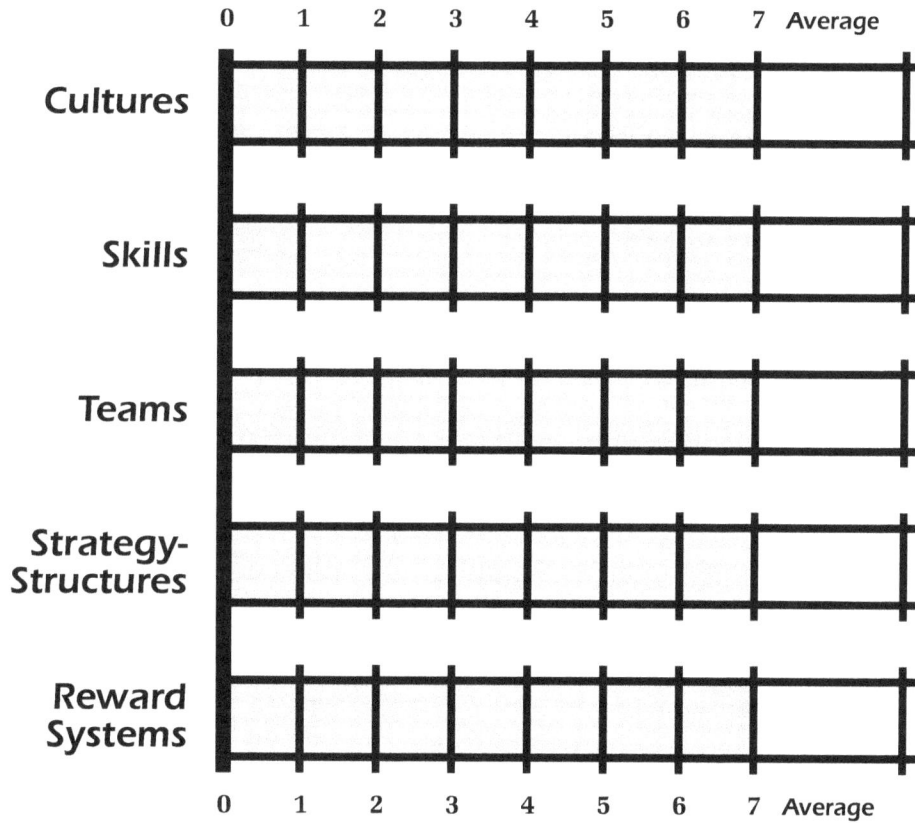

	0	1	2	3	4	5	6	7	Average
Cultures									
Skills									
Teams									
Strategy-Structures									
Reward Systems									

0	1	2	3	4	5	6	7	Average

TIME-GAP PROFILE

Defining Five Time-Gaps

People spend their time at work doing a great many things—as affected by formal and informal systems. The informal systems include how people interact with one another on the job—individually and in groups—using their behavioral styles and technical skills. The formal systems include the documents, technologies, and resources that guide what people are supposed to do. Taken together, these two systems capture all the ways in which people spend—and waste—their time in order to contribute their talent and energy to their organization.

The informal systems can be divided into three tracks to organizational success: Cultures, Skills, and Teams. The culture track enhances trust, communication, information sharing, and willingness to change among members—the necessary foundation for any organization to succeed. The skills track enhances ways for managing people and problems—so all members will use their talent efficiently and effectively. The team track infuses the cultures and skills into each group in the organization—so that cooperation, teamwork, and effective group problem solving can flourish on a daily basis.

The formal systems can be organized into two tracks to organizational success: Strategy-Structures and Reward Systems. The strategy-structure track clarifies where the organization is headed (for example, goals and objectives) and how it is designed to get there (for example, policies and procedures). Lastly, the reward system track motivates high performance by using clear performance criteria, assessing performance objectively, and delivering rewards based on performance.

FIVE TIME-GAPS
FOR THE
FIVE TRACKS

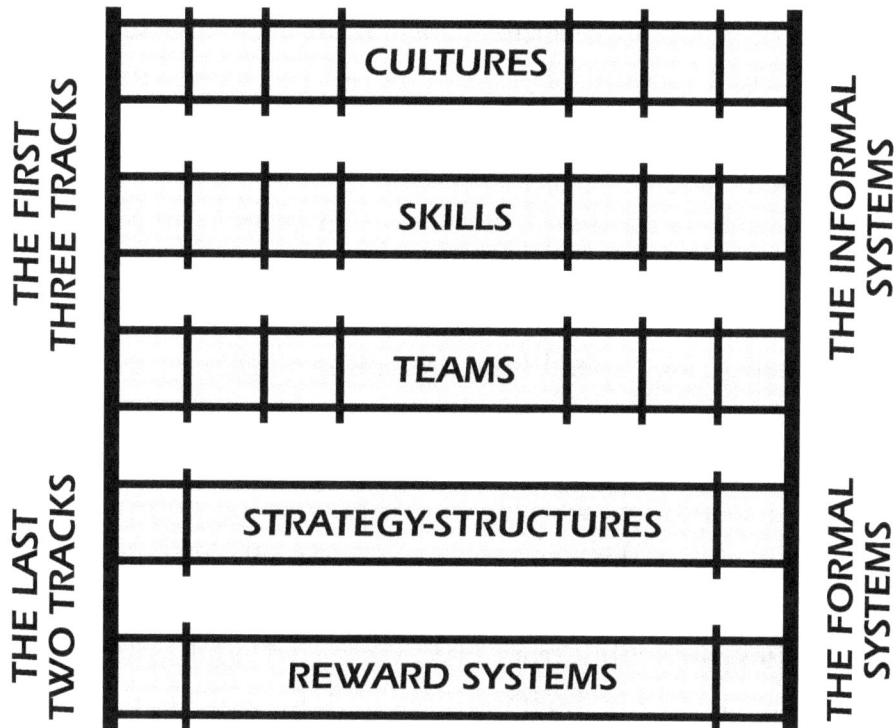

THE FIRST THREE TRACKS

THE INFORMAL SYSTEMS

| CULTURES |
| SKILLS |
| TEAMS |

THE LAST TWO TRACKS

THE FORMAL SYSTEMS

| STRATEGY-STRUCTURES |
| REWARD SYSTEMS |

Spending the Right Time
on Each Track
to Achieve
Organizational
Success

The five tracks provide a complete framework for seeing how time is spent in the pursuit of organizational goals. As shown on the preceding page, the five tracks correspond to the same five time-gaps assessed by this survey. A *time-gap* is defined as the difference between spending the right versus the wrong time on those tasks and activities that pertain to any of the five tracks—and hence any formal or informal system in the organization. As such, all five time-gaps concern whether individuals are spending the right amount of time doing all the things that determine long-term organizational success.

Cultures: Do you spend time fostering an adaptive culture, responding quickly to requests from other departments, and encouraging others to forgive past wrongdoings by moving forward with a clean slate? Or do you, deliberately or not, spend time promoting additional mistrust across departments, conveying doom-and-gloom attitudes, and bearing grudges?

Skills: Do you spend time working to clarify your job priorities, planning your work day, and sticking to the most important tasks until you have completed them? Or do you, purposely or not, spend time working on the wrong priorities, switching from task to task without bringing any job to completion, and saving the important work for another day?

Teams: Do you spend time sharing your knowledge and expertise with members of your group (including your boss), encouraging teamwork, and fostering effective problem-solving efforts? Or do you, deliberately or not, spend time keeping your good ideas to yourself, preventing the quieter members from entering into the discussion, and publicly agreeing with group decisions even though you really disagree?

Strategy-Structures: Do you spend time seeking to clarify organizational goals, objectives, and procedures with your boss *before* you pursue your daily work? Or do you, deliberately or not, spend time working on the same old things in the same old way without refocusing your priorities—even though organizational goals and objectives may be shifting?

Reward Systems: Do you spend time seeking to learn what criteria will be used to review your performance, how the review system works, and what you can do in the interim to improve your performance? Or do you, consciously or not, spend time complaining about the reward system—neither trying to understand it nor improve it?

If the precious time, and thus the talent, of individuals is being diverted from trusting other groups (Cultures), using skills to prioritize, plan, and do the work (Skills), cooperating with coworkers and the boss in order to resolve important work-group problems (Teams), focusing on the right goals and objectives with the right policies and procedures (Strategy-Structures), and pursuing clear and valid performance criteria (Reward Systems) *it will be difficult—if not impossible—for individuals and groups to contribute to their organization's goals.* While the five tracks cover the whole system of organization and, therefore, might not be under the full control of every individual, *the five time-gaps focus on just those tasks and activities that can be controlled by every person.* By finding out how precious time is being wasted the same way every day, individuals and groups can choose to redistribute their time on tasks—from spending the wrong time on the wrong tasks or the wrong time on the right tasks to the right time on the right tasks—and thereby increase their contribution to their organization's goals.

Interpreting Your Scores

Scores (and averages) for the five time-gaps can vary between 0 and 7—since there are 7 items for each score. The following diagnostic guidelines suggest what time-gaps need special attention.

Any score of 3 or higher represents a significant time-gap. Such a gap suggests that a **misallocation of time** is being spent on one of the tracks to organizational success: Cultures, Skills, Teams, Strategy-Structures, or Reward Systems. In particular, a significant time-gap represents either spending too much time on those tasks and activities that **distract** from achieving the organization's goals or spending too little time on those things that **contribute** to the organization's goals. But in either case, the individual is indicating that he or she should be spending less time or more time on that track to organizational success. A score of 2 is border-line (the significance of the gap can go either way), while a score of 1 or 0 suggests an insignificant time-gap. If three or more time-gaps are found to be significant according to these guidelines, then a rather broad-based misallocation of time is diverting the individual's potential contribution to organizational goals. In this case, *the allocation of time on a variety of tasks and activities is off track.*

These same diagnostic guidelines apply to average time-gap scores for any work group, department, or the whole organization: Any significant average score (3 or higher) suggests that time on key tasks and activities is being diverted somehow—by either spending too much or too little time on the very things that determine organizational success. Consider, for example, a work group's Time-Gap Profile on the opposite page:

Significant Time-Gaps
in the First Three Tracks

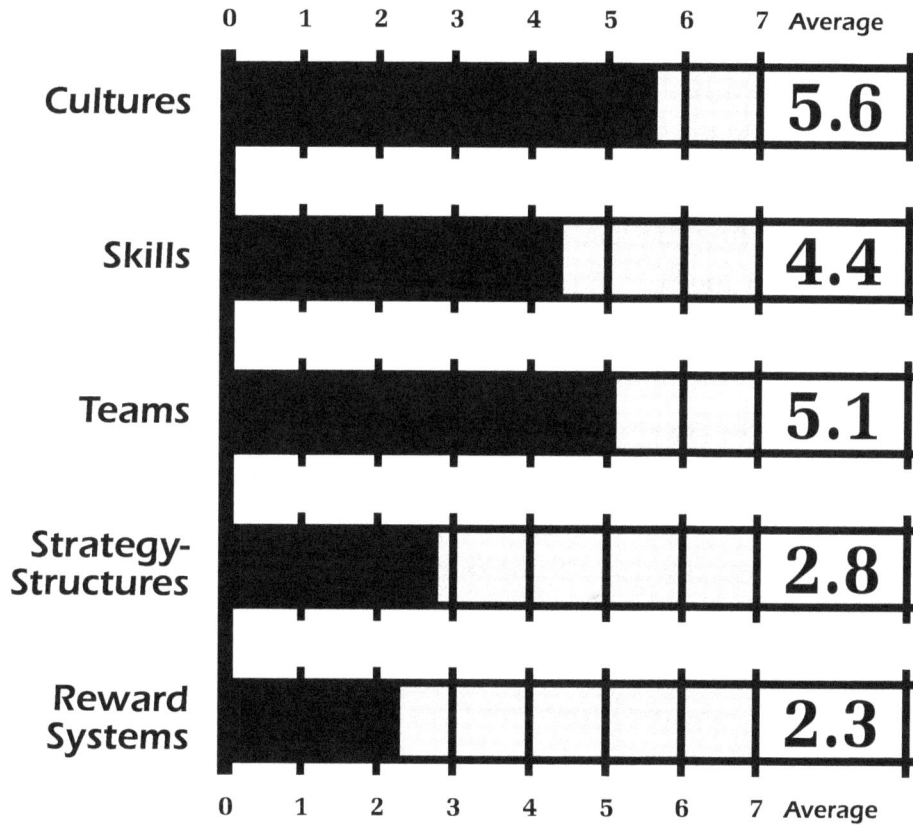

	0	1	2	3	4	5	6	7	Average
Cultures									**5.6**
Skills									**4.4**
Teams									**5.1**
Strategy-Structures									**2.8**
Reward Systems									**2.3**

TIME-GAP PROFILE

On the previous page, three significant time-gaps are identified for the work group in question—covering the first three tracks to organizational success. In this case, the work group is acknowledging that it should be spending more time promoting a healthy culture, making better use of individual skills for prioritizing and planning the work, and managing group discussions and meetings so that all the knowledge and expertise of group members is available for problem-solving efforts. In addition, the work group is acknowledging that it should be spending less time on any tasks or activities that undermine the Cultures, Skills, and Teams in the organization. Regarding the last two tracks to organizational success, however, it appears that the work group is spending the right amount of time clarifying organizational goals and objectives (Strategy-Structures) and ensuring that all group members are guided by clear performance criteria and know how the review process works (Reward Systems). While this work group seems to be managing the formal systems effectively, it is not fully utilizing its talent and energy: It may know what to do, but it is being diverted from getting the right thing done.

On the opposite page, another example reveals two significant time-gaps in the last two tracks to organizational success (with insignificant time-gaps in the first three tracks). In this case, the work group is not spending the right amount of time clarifying and understanding how the formal systems work, even though it is doing the necessary job of trust building, prioritizing and completing its daily workload, and fostering teamwork and cooperation: Thus, the work group may be developing an effective informal organization for getting the day-to-day work done, but its time will be wasted if it is getting the *wrong* work done.

Significant Time-Gaps
in the Last Two Tracks

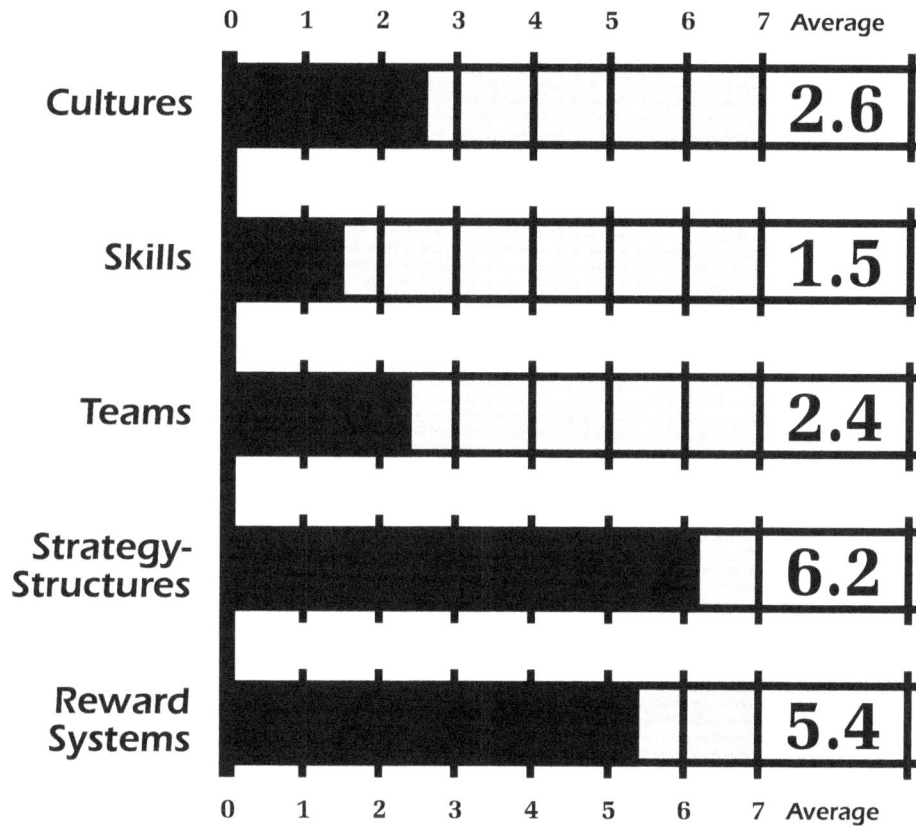

	0	1	2	3	4	5	6	7	Average
Cultures									**2.6**
Skills									**1.5**
Teams									**2.4**
Strategy-Structures									**6.2**
Reward Systems									**5.4**

TIME-GAP PROFILE

As a final example, the next page shows a Time-Gap Profile that doesn't reveal a clear pattern with respect to time-gaps in the first three tracks or the last two tracks. Rather, this work unit seems to be diverting its time across both the informal and formal organization—by not managing its culture well, not contributing to the team effort, and not having enough clarity about organizational goals and job priorities. Thus, when no clear pattern emerges, it is still important to pinpoint which particular tracks will need a reallocation of time in order for a work group to improve its contribution to organizational goals.

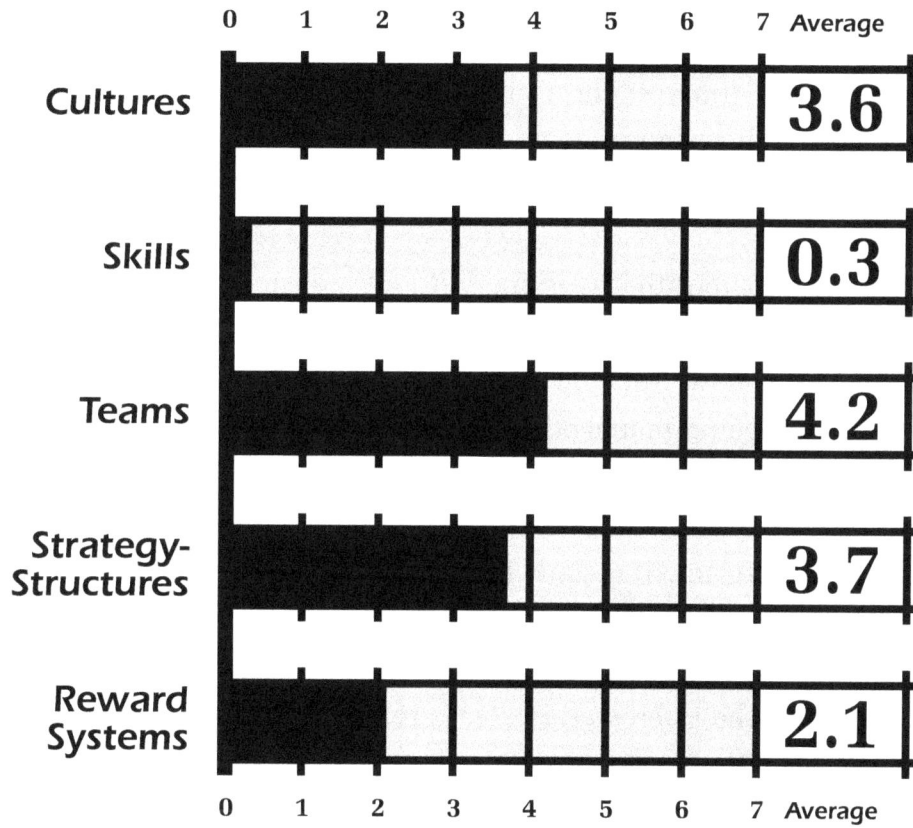

	0	1	2	3	4	5	6	7	Average
Cultures									3.6
Skills									0.3
Teams									4.2
Strategy-Structures									3.7
Reward Systems									2.1

TIME-GAP PROFILE

Closing Time-Gaps

Knowing the specific areas (tracks) in which time is being diverted from fully contributing to the organization's goals (either as individuals or in work units), we can focus attention on how time can be reallocated—from spending the wrong time on the wrong tasks or the wrong time on the right tasks to the right time on the right tasks. Such a reallocation of time will ensure that all individuals and work units are doing the right things in the right way.

It should be readily apparent that working without a clear understanding of organizational goals and objectives will severely limit the contribution of members, no matter how well the first three tracks (representing the informal systems) are being managed. And no matter how well the last two tracks are addressed (the formal systems), ineffective Cultures, Skills, and Teams will obstruct the talent and energy of the membership. Only by maintaining insignificant time-gaps in each of the five tracks can all individuals and work units fully contribute to the long-term success of their organization. For a complete discussion of the theories and methods behind the five tracks, the interested reader is referred to R. H. Kilmann, *Beyond the Quick Fix* (Washington DC: Beard, 2004) as well as *Quantum Organizations* (Newport Coast, CA: Kilmann Diagnostics, 2011).

Assessment Tools for the Eight Tracks
Distributed by Kilmann Diagnostics

Kilmann-Saxton Culture-Gap® Survey

Kilmanns Organizational Belief Survey

Kilmanns Time-Gap Survey

Kilmanns Team-Gap Survey

Organizational Courage Assessment

Kilmann-Covin Organizational Influence Survey

Plus the Online Version of the

Thomas-Kilmann Conflict Mode Instrument

Plus These Training and Development Tools

Work Sheets for Identifying and Closing Culture-Gaps

Work Sheets for Identifying and Closing Team-Gaps

And the Book That Fully Explains the Eight Tracks

Quantum Organizations